PREFACE

Any study of Welsh samplers must begin by drawing attention to the work of Ffransis G. Payne, former Keeper at the Welsh Folk Museum, and his excellent *Guide to the Collection of Samplers and Embroideries.* Published in 1939, this remains a standard work of reference for anyone studying the history of samplers.

When the *Guide* was published, the Museum's collection comprised some 180 samplers. A few had been acquired during the early years of this century, but the broad base of the collection was established in 1920 with the purchase of fifty-eight samplers from Edward Lovett, a noted English antiquarian and folklorist, who had close connections with the National Museum of Wales. The quality and variety of the collection was further enhanced by the Alderman C. F. Sanders donation of 1936 which included the two oldest samplers in our collection.

Since 1939 the number of samplers held by the Welsh Folk Museum has more than doubled and now stands at over 430. Most of these are of Welsh origin, although very few have inscriptions in the Welsh language. There are also many excellent comparative specimens from England, Belgium and Holland, together with isolated examples from Germany, Italy, Switzerland and Ireland. They range in date from the middle of the seventeenth century to the mid twentieth century, covering a timespan of some three hundred years.

The aim of this booklet is threefold. Firstly, it is intended to provide access to at least a small part of this superb collection, only a selecti[illegible]h can be on pub[illegible]cond place, to g[illegible]ous types of sa[illegible]e skill and indust[illegible] made them. Fina[illegible] those who own h[illegible] worked mo[illegible]ture generations [illegible]onservator of the Welsh Folk Museum, Miss Mair Rees, has compiled comprehensive notes on the cleaning, mounting and framing of samplers, as well as the conditions under which they should be displayed and stored.

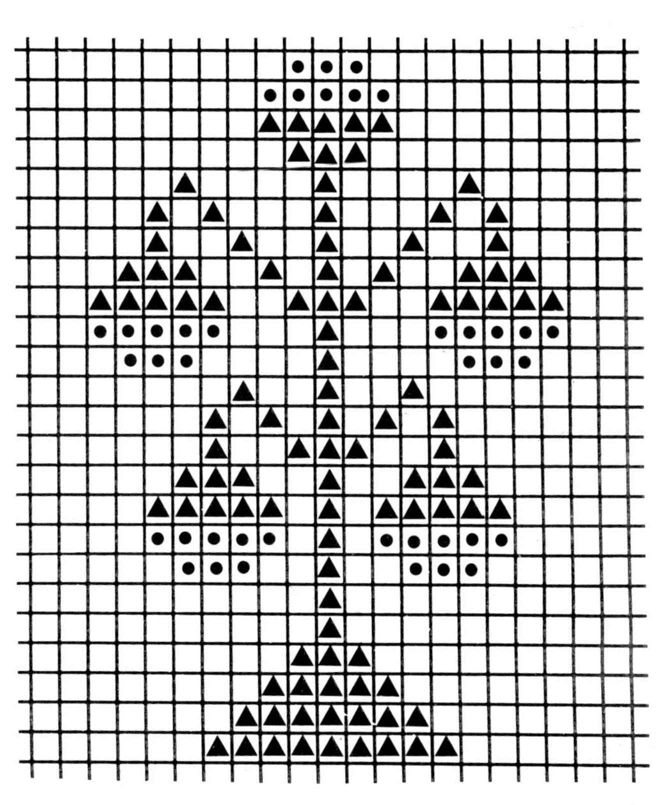

USE OF THE SAMPLER

Most people, if asked to describe the appearance of a sampler, would mention an alphabet, motifs of flowers and animals, perhaps a house, and certainly the name and age of a young child, all sewn in cross stitch. This, however, is far from the original appearance of what we know now as a sampler. The very first 'examples' or samplers were random collections of stitches and patterns kept by women as a reference 'book' at a time when published pattern books were not readily available.

From the late medieval period, and probably earlier, when embroidered decoration became popular on clothing and soft furnishings, women recorded useful patterns on their samplers, adding new ones as they encountered them. These pieces of linen were never intended for display, but were usually kept rolled up in a work box. Samplers of this type were certainly known in Wales as early as the fifteenth century. In a poem of this period, Tudur Aled of Llansannan, Clwyd, wrote *Aur wniadau a'r nydwydd / arfer o'r sampler yw'r swydd [Golden stitches with the needle / the use of the sampler is the work.]* No known

Seventeenth century English sampler, embroidered on linen with coloured silks in chain, cross, double-faggot, eyelet and satin stitch, and including two bands of cut and drawn-thread work filled with needlepoint stitches.

Welsh examples of this early type have survived, although some continental samplers of sixteenth century date are preserved in the Victoria and Albert Museum in London.

As printed pattern books became more common, the original use of the sampler declined. Samplers began to be used for teaching needlework to young girls; the repetition of stitches and designs not only provided sewing practice, but also resulted in a decorative testimonial to their skill. Border patterns and other repeated motifs were arranged in horizontal bands on long, narrow strips of linen. Letters of the alphabet and numerals, useful as patterns for marking household linen or items of clothing, came to be included during the seventeenth century. Most contain a variety of different stitches. The earliest dated example in the Museum collection is an English sampler made by Katherine Manning in 1659, which contains cross, satin, chain, eyelet and double faggot stitches as well as bands of cut and drawn-thread work. Another, dated 1699, is worked entirely in cut and drawn-thread work, filled with various patterns in needlepoint stitches.

Lettering and numerals were almost exclusively worked in cross and eyelet stitches on the eighteenth century examples, but other stitches used in motifs are herringbone, stem, split and backstitch, as well as the more common cross and satin stitch.

Most nineteenth century samplers could be said to be of the decorative rather than utilitarian type, and the range of stitches gradually decreased until cross stitch had become so universal that it was known as the sampler stitch. Exceptions to this are the fine darning samplers which were still being made during the last century, several continental examples of which survive in the museum collections. The middle years of the nineteenth century also saw a revival of the original use of the sampler in woolwork, with random examples of patterns containing Florentine, tent and other stitches, perhaps collected in order to test colour combinations for later use. One of the examples of this type in the Museum collection even reproduces the long, narrow format of the earlier era.

Sampler of English origin, embroidered with white linen thread on unbleached linen in satin and backstitch, with six panels of cut and drawn-thread work.

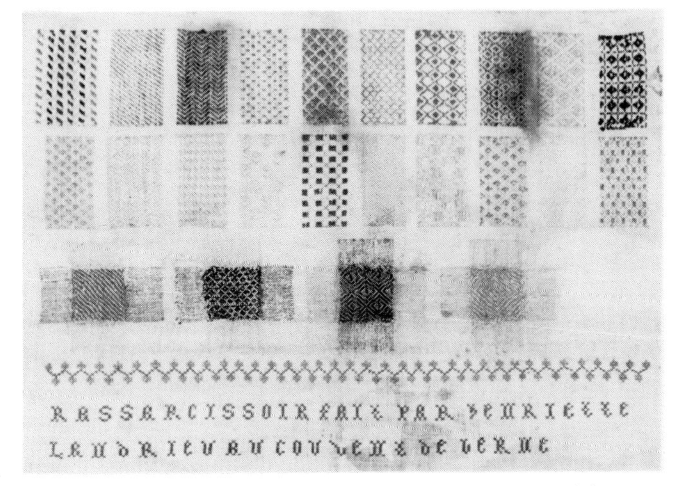

Swiss sampler, embroidered with coloured silks in darning and cross stitches, and including rectangles of pattern darning and four crosses with portions cut out and closely darned; of early nineteenth century date.

Nineteenth century random woolwork sampler, worked with coloured wools on unbleached linen, from Rhyl, Clwyd.

Sampler, c. 1700, embroidered with coloured silks on linen in cross stitch; there are thirteen bands of geometric and stylized floral motifs, with a border of three narrow stripes.

Embroidery stitches found on samplers

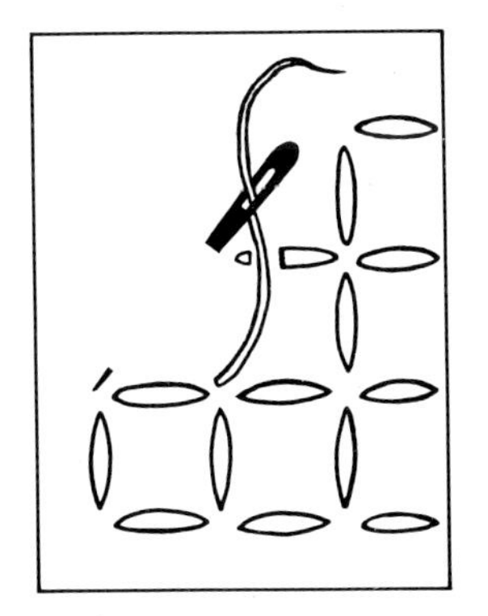

Single Faggot

Eyelet

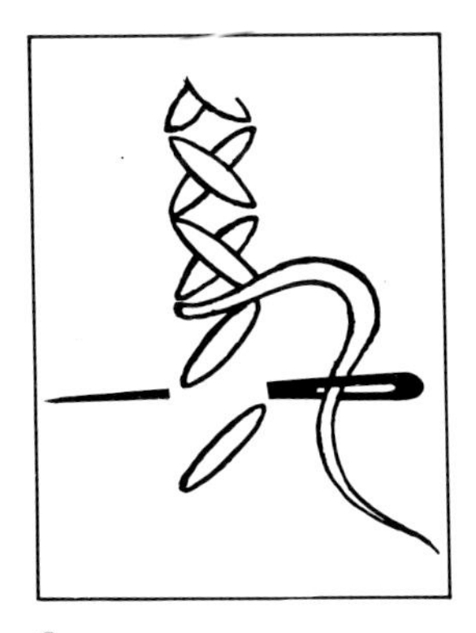

Cross

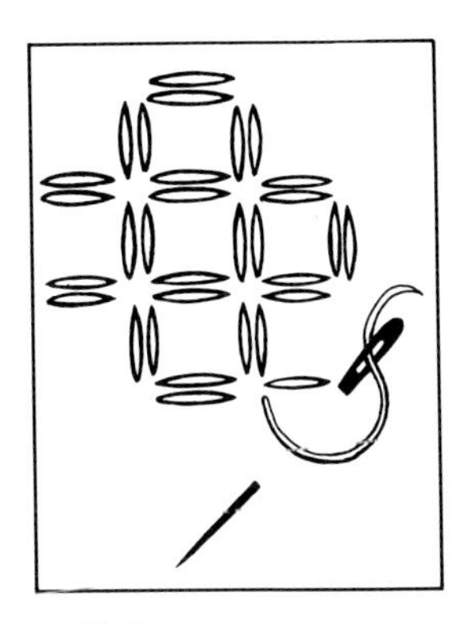

Double Faggot

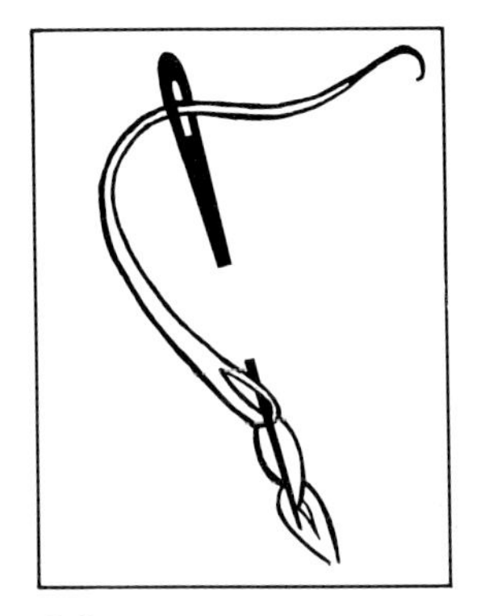

Split

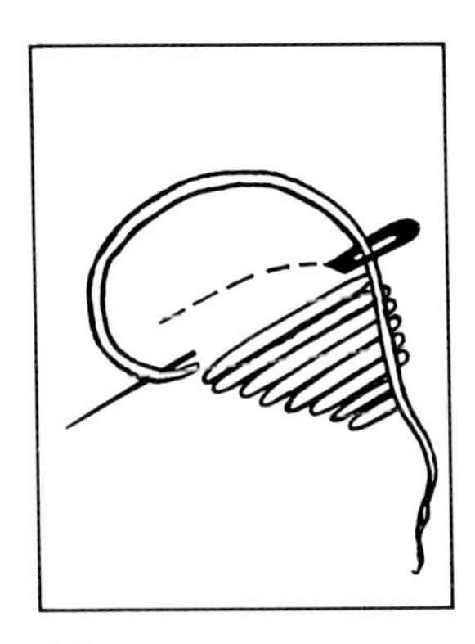

Satin

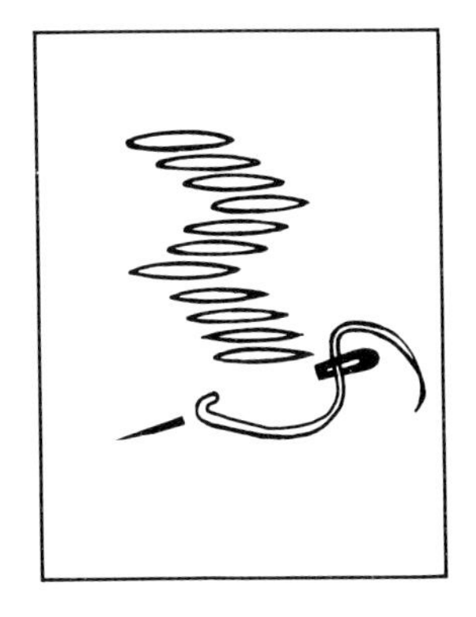

Florentine

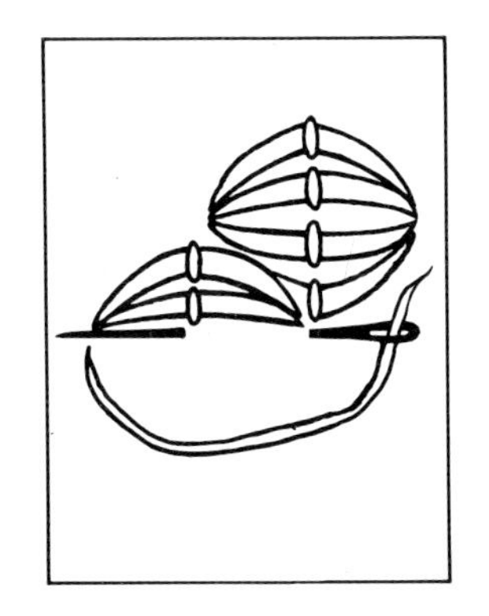

Rococco

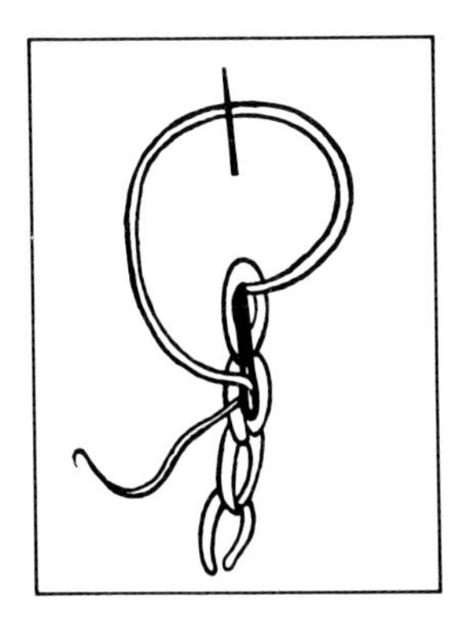

Chain

SAMPLER MOTIFS AND DESIGNS

making birds with a needle

There is a remarkable continuity in the types of designs and motifs used on samplers over the centuries, due in great part to the lack of originality of the later sampler makers. The origins of many of these designs lie in the embroidery patterns popular throughout Europe during the fifteenth and sixteenth centuries. A comparison of the motifs found on German, Dutch and Belgian samplers with those from Wales and other parts of the British Isles shows more points of similarity than difference.

Embroidery designs used in Wales have been well described by poets of the period. Lewis Glyn Cothi, for example, whose works date from the middle of the fifteenth century, described embroidered cloths and curtains as being *full of designs - saplings, leaves, figures, birds of the earth, lions ... stags and cross designs*...and so on. Elsewhere, the same poet describes a coverlet full of *minute designs, the work of a maiden's hands, oak trees and figures of birds of the forest.* Another poet, Gruffudd ab Ieuan ap Llywelyn Fychan at the turn of the sixteenth century wrote *You are one who would make birds with a needle.* Still later, in the seventeenth century, Huwcyn Sion described a collar as being embroidered with *a picture of every bird beneath the heavens and every fish in the sea.*

It is possible that some of these designs may have been drawn from nature, but most, especially the more exotic animals and biblical subjects, must have been copied from illuminated manuscripts or simply

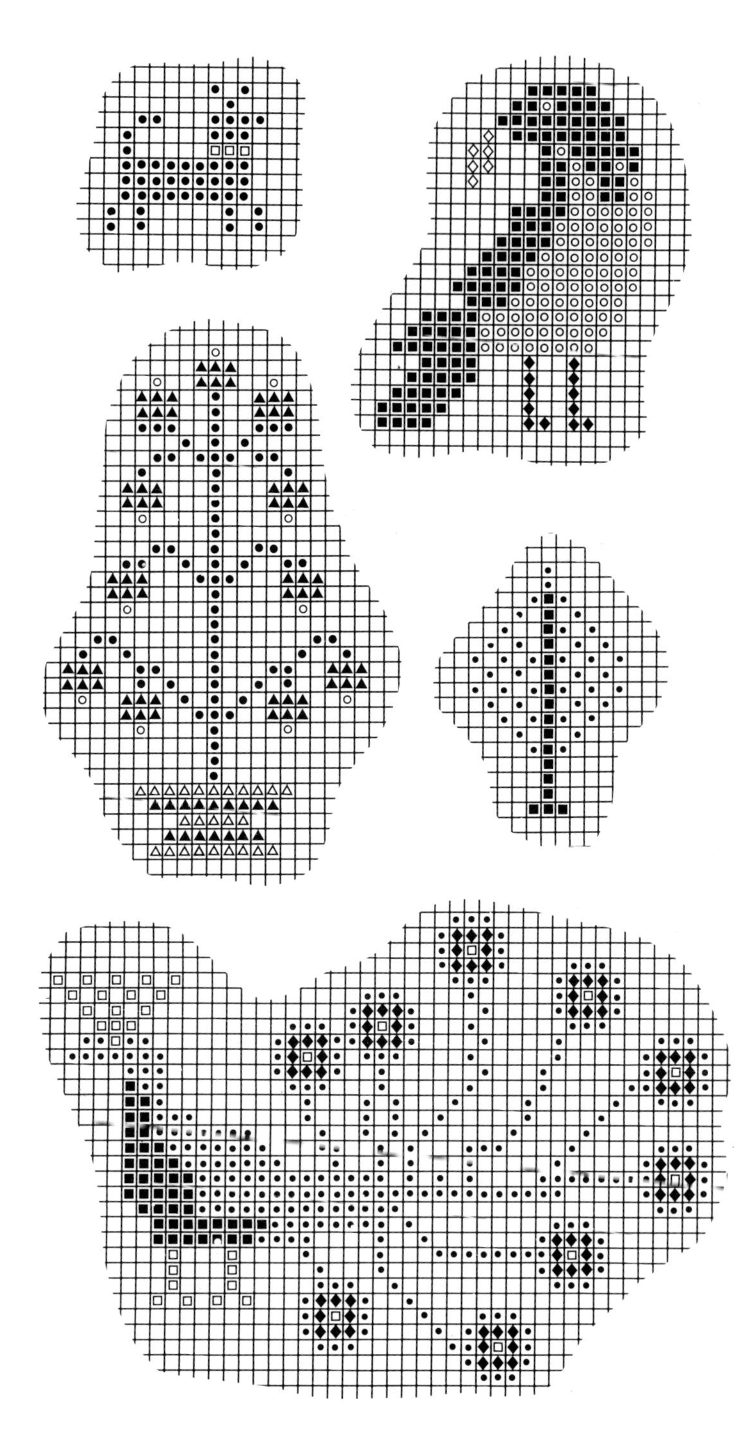

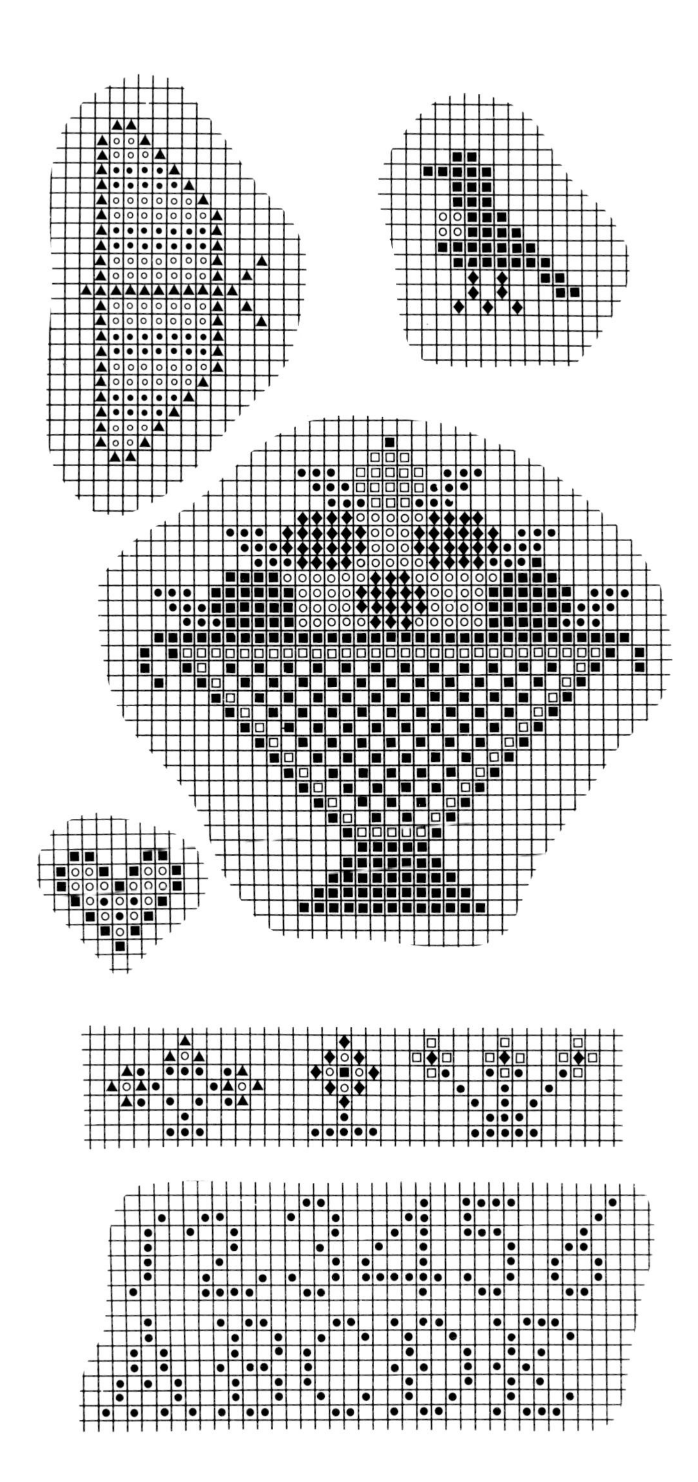

from other embroideries or tapestries. During the sixteenth century, some patterns were certainly copied from the printed books now beginning to appear, many of which originally came from Germany and Italy.

The long narrow format of seventeenth century samplers imposed a formal, highly stylized type of motif, arranged in horizontal bands. These motifs are mainly geometric and floral, though figures do appear. The stylized birds, animals, trees and flowers, and others such as crowns and hearts, continued to be copied and re-copied throughout the eighteenth and nineteenth centuries. As the samplers came to be regarded as decorative rather than utilitarian items, narrow geometric borders began to be used. Later, more decorative border patterns were borrowed from the horizontal rows of the long, narrow samplers and the stereotyped design of zig-zag or wavy lines interspersed with strawberries, acorns or flowers developed.

This change to a more pictorial format, undoubtedly influenced by the popularity of silk embroidered pictures, resulted in the use of a more naturalistic style of bird and flower motifs usually executed in satin stitch. These were especially popular during the 1830s and 1840s, and although they appear to be more spontaneous than the stylized cross-stitch motifs, the same designs can be seen repeated on a variety of samplers. This repetition is most frequently, and perhaps understandably, found on products from the same school, where pupils are obviously copying from a set example provided by the teacher. For instance, there are three samplers in the collection from Bedwas school, Mid Glamorgan, which range in date from 1842 to 1849, all of which have virtually identical floral motifs.

Some other motifs which survived the centuries were figures such as Adam and Eve, often depicted with the Tree of Life and the serpent. Buildings, too, were popular subjects, which could easily be worked in cross stitch and adapted to represent the worker's own home. The most popular style was the four-square Georgian house, which remained virtually unchanged on samplers throughout the nineteenth century despite the vagaries of Victorian architecture. Other buildings depicted were churches, windmills and even conservatories.

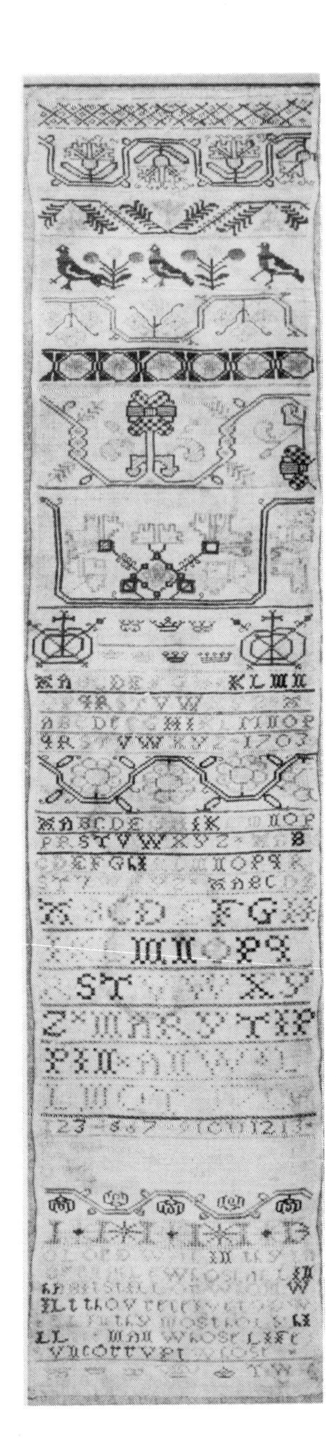

Finely embroidered sampler, worked with coloured silks in cross and satin stitch on muslin. It contains a large collection of traditional motifs; the inclusion of sailing ships may be due to the fact that it was made at the port of Holyhead in Anglesey.

Sampler with bands of bird and flower motifs done mainly in cross and stem stitches, with alphabet and inscription in eye stitch.
The inscription reads: 1703 MARY TIPPITT AN WILMOT 1704.

Dutch sampler, dated 1819, worked with coloured silks in cross stitch on linen; there are many motifs in common with British samplers, including the stag, peacock and Adam and Eve figures.

Some sampler makers introduced an element of originality by attempting to reproduce actual buildings, such as Welshpool Church, St. David's Cathedral and Glansevern Hall. A sampler depicting Penrhyn Castle, however, is of a quite different category. This is typical of many samplers whose motifs are derived from the published patterns for Berlin woolwork which first became widespread during the 1840s and whose popularity steadily increased. There is in fact a Berlin woolwork picture in the Museum collection on which the maker has used the same pattern of Penrhyn Castle. Other popular woolwork designs depicted naturalistic motifs of birds and flowers, biblical scenes or copies of paintings. These motifs were used indiscriminately by the sampler makers side by side with more traditional motifs and borders.

Sampler embroidered with coloured silks on woollen canvas in cross stitch. The central motif represents Adam and Eve with the Tree of Life. From Cardiff.

Sampler of woollen canvas embroidered with coloured silks in a variety of stitches, including cross, chain and satin stitch. From South Wales.

Sampler dated 1833 embroidered in cross stitch with coloured silks on woollen canvas; the motifs are arranged in bands and include a typical sampler house. From Llangynidr, Powys.

Sampler, c. 1900. embroidered on cotton canvas with brightly coloured wools in cross stitch. From Hirwaun, Mid Glamorgan.

Mid nineteenth century canvas sampler embroidered with coloured silks in cross, satin and chain stitch; the motifs are of the woolwork type. From Swansea, West Glamorgan.

Woolwork-type sampler, embroidered with coloured wools on canvas, with both English and .Welsh inscriptions. From Aberporth, Dyfed.

SAMPLER INSCRIPTIONS AND VERSES

here you may see my name complete

In the seventeenth century, samplers generally had no inscription other than an alphabet and numerals together with the maker's name or intitials and the date. At this time, samplers were still an adult product, but as more young girls began to make samplers it became popular to record the child's age as further evidence of her skill. It appears that this practicc rebounded on many young ladies at a later date when they discovered that their childhood work revealed their present age, and there are a number of samplers with either age or date unpicked.

During the eighteenth and early nineteenth centuries the amount of lettering increased, and as well as various styles of alphabet, moral phrases and verses became popular. In some cases, the samplers were comprised completely of verses, with decoration being reduced to a narrow geometric border. One sampler in the collection, made in 1797, consists only of three verses, one of which is the popular *Life of the Happy Man* (see opposite). It has a very slight border and no other decorative elements, and is very similar in construction to the well-known samplers embroidered by the Bronte sisters at the later date of 1829-30. Verse samplers of this type were usually executed in black silk, and the verse itself was inevitably of a moral nature. This particular sampler is unusual in that it ends with a Christmas verse, with

Martha Brimble Hailse November the 2x 1797

The LIFE OF The HAPPY MAN.
The Happy Man was Born in the City of Regeneration
In the parish Of Repentance unto Life was Educated at the
School of Obedience and now Lives in the plain of
perseverance he work at the Trade of Diligence.
Notwithstanding he has A large Estate in the County Of
Christian Contentment and many Times does jobs Of
Self-denial He wears the plain Garment of Humility and has
A better Suit to put on when he goes to Court call'd the
Robe of CHRISTs Righteousness He often walks in the
Valley of Self-abasement and Sometimes Climbs the
Mountain of Spiritual Mindedness Breakfasts Every
Morning upon Spiritual prayer And sups Every Evening
Upon the Same he has Meat to eat Which the World knows
Not of and his Drink is the Sincere Milk of the Word.
Thus happy he Lives And Happy he Dies.
Happy is he who has Gospel Submission in his Will due
Orde in his Affections Sound peace in his Conscience.
Sanctifying Grace in his Soul real Divinity in his Breast.
True Humility in his Heart the Redeemers Yoke on his Neck
A vain World under his Feet and A Crown of Glory on his
Head—Happy is the Life of such A Man—In order to
Attain which is to pray fervently Believe firmly wait
patiently Work abundantly Live holy Die daily Watch your
Hearts guard your Senses Redeem your Time Love
CHRIST and Long for GLORY

To be Happy is not Only to Enjoy the pleasures of Sense
But peace and Tranquility of Mind
I Laid me down And Slept And Rose up Again for the Lord
Sustained me praised be his holy Name for Ever & Ever Amen

At the Nativity of CHRIST our LORD
The Angels did Rejoice with one Accord
Let Christmas Imitate Them heare on Earth
And keep this Feast with joy And Civil Mirth.
Sarah Newton Wraxall her Christmas piece December the 26
In the year of our LORD 1797 Age'd 10 Years

the inscription *Sarah Newton Wraxall her Christmas piece December the 26 ... 1797 Age'd 10 years,* although a different name, place and date appear at the head.

Few other samplers in the collection refer to specific church or calendar events. The verses tend rather to general exhortations to live a virtuous, industrious and religious life. There are many examples containing references to the bee, one example, dated 1778, begins

How doth the little busy bee
Improve each shining hour

and similarly, from 1808,

The busy bee with ceaseless hum
Morn, noon and evening sucks the flowers

Other verses dealing with the benefits of industry also illuminate the eighteenth century view of women, stating in 1727 that *Reading good books and needlework should be their whole felicity* (see page 17), and in a later example, dated 1782,

Industry taught in early days
Not only gives the Teacher praise
But gives us Pleasure when we view
the work that Innocence can do...
Go on my dear strive to excell
Improve in work and reading well
For book and needle both command
To make a Housewife and a Friend.

Virtue and sin were also frequently subjects of verses, such as *The paths of virtue lead to peace, The ways of sin - to death* and *Virtue's the chiefest Beauty of the mind, the noblest Ornament of human kind.* The value of religion seems never to have been far from the embroiderer's thoughts, one of the most popular verses being:

Tis religion that can give
Sweetest pleasure while we live
Tis religion must supply
Solid comforts when we die.

Sampler embroidered in chain, cross, flat and stem stitches on woollen canvas, using coloured silks. From Cardiff.

Unusual sampler, embroidered on unbleached linen using coloured silks and metallic threads. Coloured wax is also used on some of the floral motifs. Among the various stitches used are cross, Floretine, rococco, satin and stem stitch as well as couched stitch and bullion knots. From Cardiff.

Many of the nineteenth century verses advocate the study of religion to *fit us for declining age, and for the silent tomb.* These may appear extremely morbid to modern eyes, but others are even more startling, with such lines as

> *When I am dead and in my grave*
> *And all my bones are wrotten*

In another version, the same verse is completed:

> *Tho greedy worms my body eat*
> *Here you may see my name complete.*

Despite the high rate of infant mortality, reflected in the verse on a sampler from S. Westbrook's School, Pontypool, (illustrated on page 21) these seem to be rather grim verses for a sewing mistress to set young children. Whether the intention was to instil fear or philosophy is a moot question.

Biblical verses were used on many samplers, a particular favourite being the verse from Ecclesiastes Chapter 12 beginning, *Remember now thy Creator in the days of thy youth ...* This appears first on a sampler dated 1768 and on many others in the collection throughout the 19th century in both its English and its Welsh forms. Other biblical quotations commonly used are the Ten Commandments, verses from Corinthians, the Book of Proverbs, and the Psalms. The Lord's Prayer and the Creed are also quoted in full on samplers in the collection.

Among many verses invoking the name of Christ, one in particular appears on literally dozens of samplers (the earliest being 1804), though often only the first four lines are used:

> *Jesus! Permit thy gracious name to stand*
> *As the first effort of an infant hand,*
> *And while my fingers on the Canvas move*
> *Engage my tender heart to seek thy love*
> *With thy dear children let me have a part*
> *And write thy name thyself upon my heart.*

Wool-embroidered sampler on canvas, with the inscription worked in black silk. From the Swansea Valley, West Glamorgan.

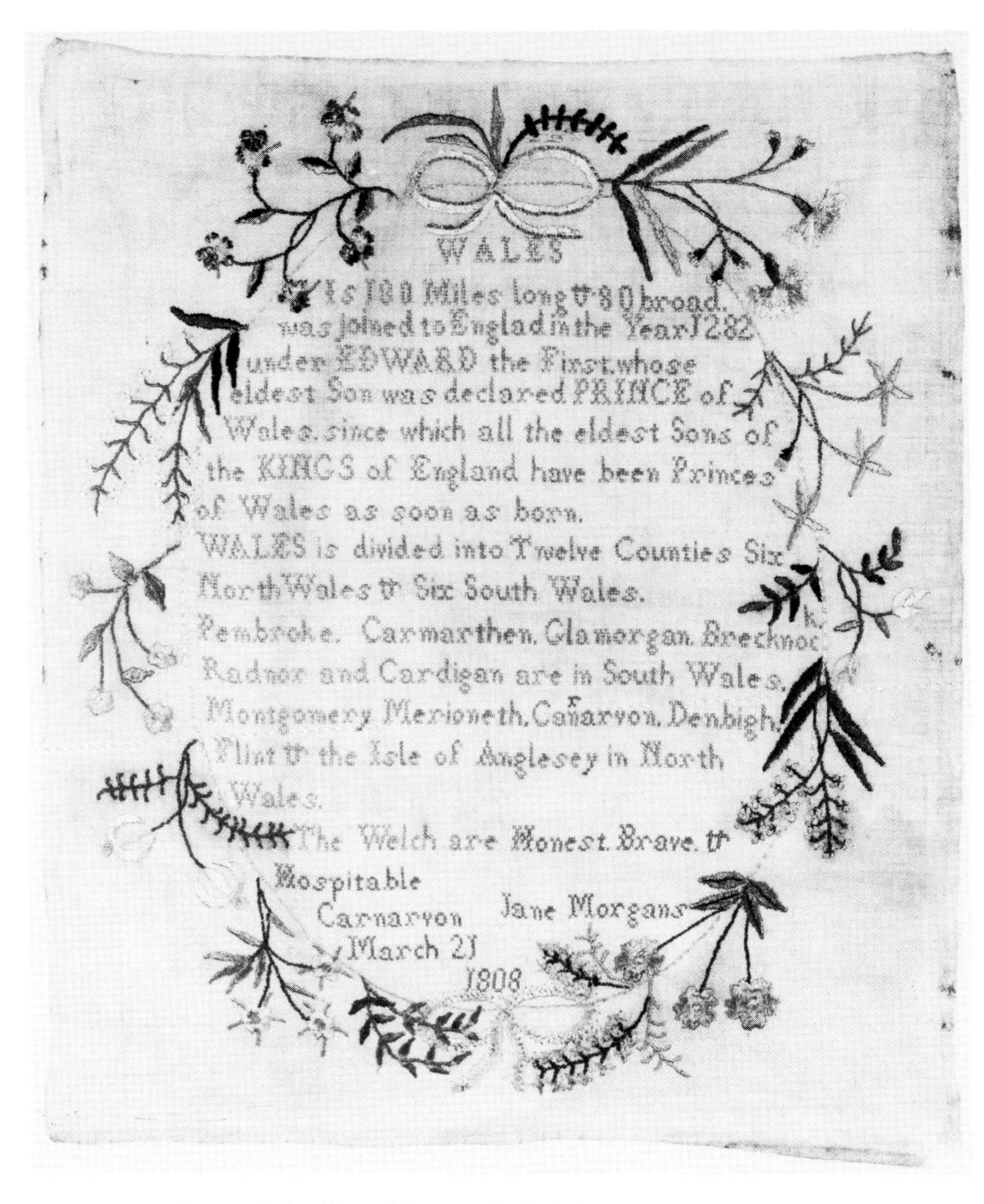

Sampler consisting of a geographical and historical description of Wales, border embroidered with coloured silks on linen, using satin, stem and cross stitches.

SAMPLERS MADE IN SCHOOLS

industry taught in early days

Many samplers surviving from the late eighteenth and nineteenth centuries were the products of schoolchildren. There have been suggestions that this was an alphabet learning device, similar to the horn book, alphabet plate or chapbook. Indeed, some miniature samplers resemble strongly the appearance of a hornbook (see opposite). However, not all school samplers include the entire alphabet, and many were by girls old enough to have known their letters. It seems more likely, therefore, that school samplers were an exercise in stitching, which was also incidentally useful in practising lettering and instilling moral precepts. The three samplers from Bedwas school have no alphabet, but consist of floral and bird motifs and verses and were embroidered by girls aged ten, eleven and seventeen years. Sarah Jane Games was aged fourteen when she completed her elaborately decorated sampler at Mrs. Jones' Seminary, Pontypridd (see page 27).The youngest child whose age is marked on a sampler was Mary Ann Hughes, aged six, and there are at least four others completed at the age of seven. However, the majority of school samplers were made by pupils between the ages of ten and fourteen.

A child's first basic sampler was usually of plain stitching in red cotton thread. One of this type in the collection, done on a loosely woven woollen canvas, entirely in cross stitch, consists of upper and lower case alphabets and the inscription: *Mabel Symons Standard 4 Splotland Board School.* When this had been completed satisfactorily, the child would then progress to finer work.

Miniature alphabet sampler, shown actual size, embroidered in cross stitch with red linen thread on fine linen canvas.
From Ty Glyn, Ciliau Aeron, Dyfed.

School sampler embroidered in cross stitch with red cotton on woollen canvas.

School sampler, embroidered on woollen canvas in coloured silks. Various stitches are used, including satin and stem, cross stitch, laid and dot stitch and French knots. From Pontypool, Gwent.

Needlework formed a large part of the syllabus for girls. Indeed, in many Welsh schools girls were taught their three Rs in the mornings and the rest of the day was spent sewing. In the Education Commissioners' Report of 1848, the inspector's report on a girl's school in Pembroke states: *The afternoons are entirely given up to sewing, excepting the teachers* [i.e. pupil teachers] *who sew with the rest from half past 1 to 3, and from 3 to 4 cipher and write.*

In poorer areas, materials were usually provided by a local benefactress, such as a landowner or vicar's wife. At St. Fagans, for example, the school master noted in his logbook in 1881 that Mrs. Davidson, the Castle housekeeper, *came to school to see about providing some sewing for the poorer children.* It is, however, the exhibition pieces which have survived to display the skill, or otherwise, of the children. While many school samplers are attractive and well made, much of the work is repetitive and lacking in originality, and, in the case of some examples from the latter part of the nineteenth century, very poorly executed.

Even as early as the 1820s, sampler making in schools was regarded by many as a mechanical process, showing little or no originality in design or use of stitches. There is a description of a dame's school in Mary Russell Mitford's *Our Village,* first published in 1819: *There are seven girls now in the school working samplers to be framed. 'Such a waste of silk, and time, and trouble!' I said to Mrs. Smith, and Mrs. Smith said to me....and then she sent for one, which in spite of her declaration that her girls never finished anything, was quite completed (probably with a good deal of her assistance), and of which, notwithstanding her rational objection to its uselessness, Lucy was not a little proud.*

Not surprisingly, the better work tends to be that produced by older girls, who may have been preparing to go into service, in which case an ability to sew neatly and mark and repair linen was an important accomplishment. The Commissioners' Report of 1848 confirms that this aim was certainly kept in mind at some schools. For example, at the free school, Llanwrda, Dyfed, *the late master's wife had been in the habit ...of teaching sewing and knitting to such of the girls in the neighbourhood as were of an age to go out to service.*

School sampler, embroidered with brightly coloured silks on woollen canvas using various stitches including satin, stem and cross stitch. From Bedwas, Mid Glamorgan.

A different type of sampler, of use to these girls and also to pupil teachers who would go on to teach needlework, was the plain-sewing sampler. This often took the form of a cotton half-sleeve upon which were displayed as many stitching, patching and darning techniques as possible. Squares of plain cream flannel were also used for this purpose. Pupil teachers kept a folio of different plain-sewing samplers for future use in lessons. Occasionally these included items of clothing worked in miniature, which are now often mistaken for doll's clothes. The earliest examples of this type in the collection date from the 1830s, and the most recent were made during the present century.

Map samplers were at the height of their popularity during the late eighteenth and early nineteenth centuries, and may well have provided the dual purpose of a geography lesson and sewing practice. Certainly some were made in schools, though many of the earlier examples, sewn on satin, owe more to the fashion for silk embroidered pictures than to the sampler tradition. The majority depict the entire British Isles, and many of these are sewn on to already printed fabric. A few in the collection, such as one made by Mary Jones at Welshpool Board School in 1810, show an outline map of Wales. Biblical maps were also made, combining a lesson in sewing, geography and scripture.

Finally, it appears that some children at least appreciated their teacher's efforts, for one sampler in the collection has the following dedication embroidered in the centre: *Presented to Miss C. C. Batho by some of the girls of Trinity School as a [...] to her of their gratitude for her kind attention to their needlework during 4 months. August 1850.*

Map sampler, embroidered with silk and chenille on satin fabric using various laid stitches; made at Pool Boarding School, Welshpool, Powys.

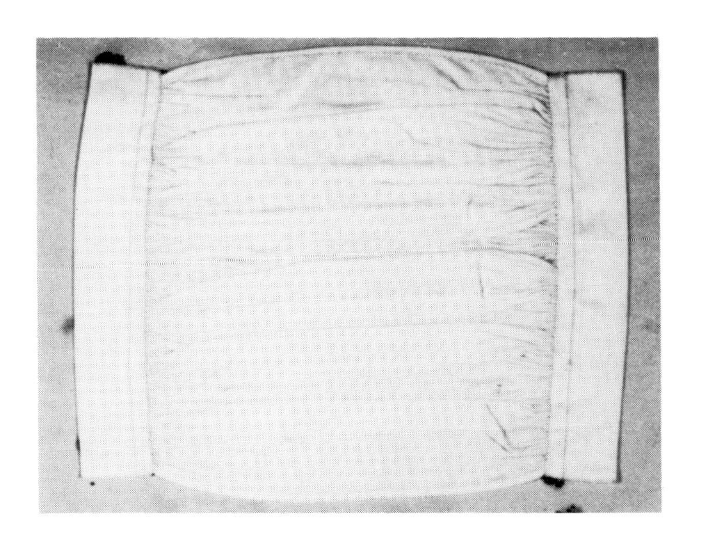

Plain sewing sampler, part of a bound album of children's needlework, c. 1838.

FAMILY AND MEMORIAL SAMPLERS

One group of samplers were made in the home rather than in school and recorded family events - births, marriages and, especially, deaths. Some of these provide a complete family tree. One early example in the collection was made by Susan Slater in 1709 and lists the dates of birth of her whole family from 1666 to 1708. Another records the family of Ellis and Mary Jones of Coedtalog, Gwynedd, giving the names and dates of birth of their fourteen children together with the dates of the deaths of the parents in 1802 and 1807 respectively (see opposite). A more decorative example of this type is one completed by ten-year-old Hannah Cook, youngest member of the Cook family. This includes Hannah herself, her parents and her six brothers and sisters, one of which rejoices in the name Asenath, together with neat floral motifs in cross stitch and an acorn and oakleaf border.

Memorial samplers perform a similar function to the mourning cards which were so common during the Victorian period and early twentieth century. Many consist only of a record of the death and burial of the deceased, but others include a memorial verse. This is often from the Bible, such as the verse from Job: *Man dieth and wasteth away; yea, man giveth up the ghost, and then where is he?,* which is worked on a sampler dedicated to the memory of John Perry and his four children, all of whom died between 1818 and 1845. Others have verses referring to the deceased. One sampler dedicated to the memory of a fourteen-year-old child is inscribed:

Do not ask me if we miss him
There is such a vacant place
Never more to hear his footsteps
Nor to see his smiling face.

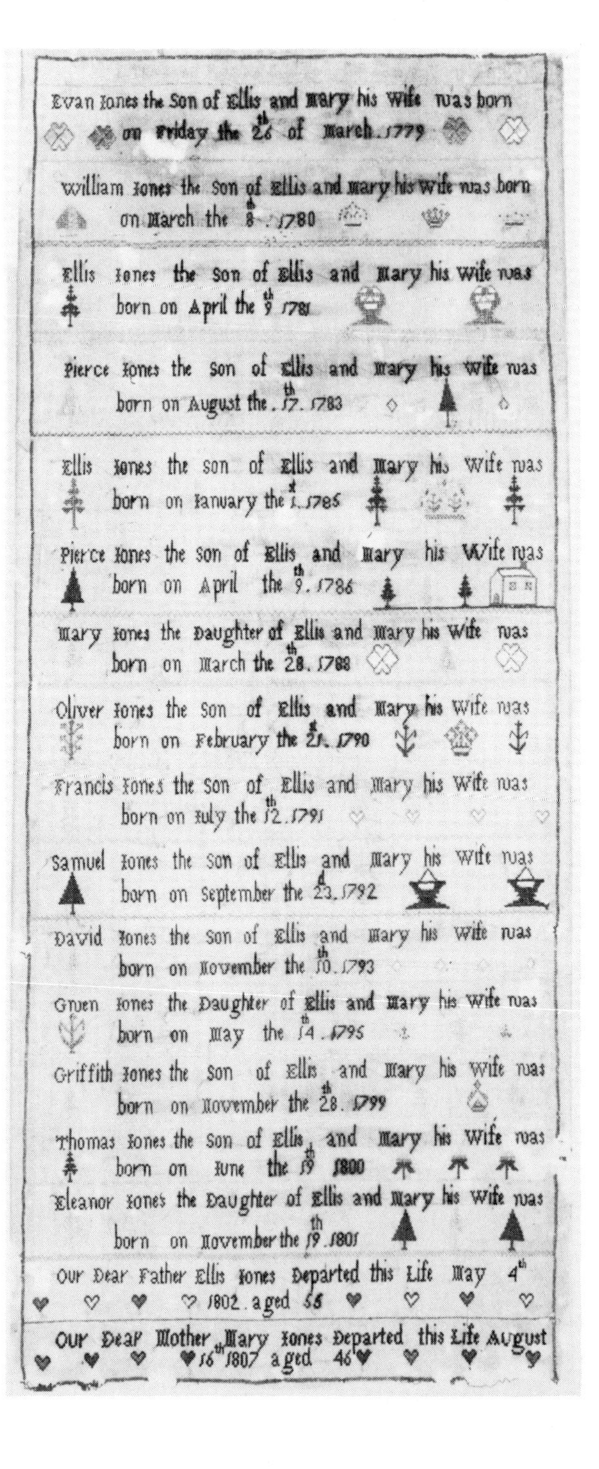

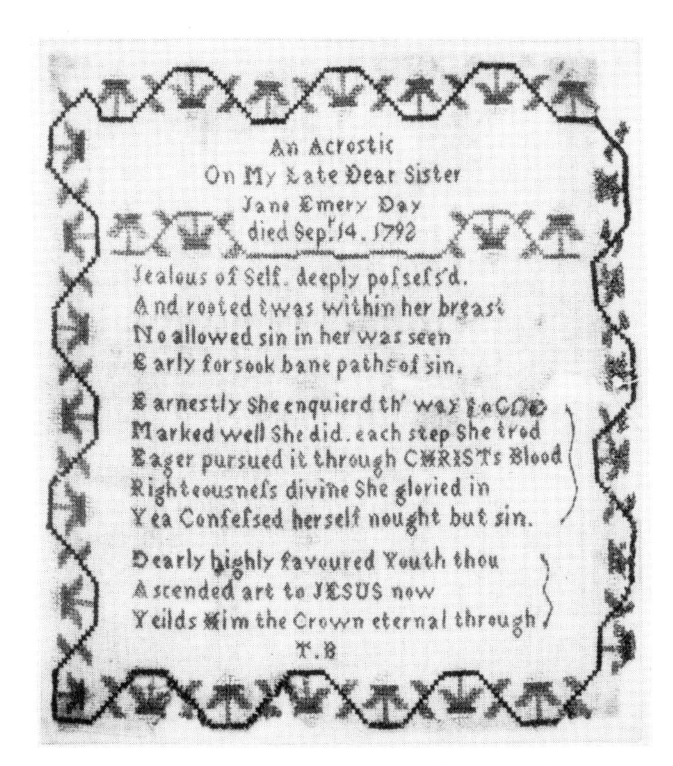

Miniature memorial sampler embroidered in coloured silks on woollen canvas.

Sampler dedicated to the maker's parents, embroidered in various flat stitches and cross stitch with coloured silks on woollen canvas.

These verses are usually of a general nature, but there is one in the collection, dated 1792, which was specially composed for the maker's sister in the form of an acrostic, the first letter of each line spelling out the dead girl's name, Jane Emery Day (see above).

One member of the Davies family of Llanfyllin, Powys, went to the extent of completing five separate samplers to the memory of John Osborne Davies, one of which is dated 1902.

Gift samplers actually inscribed as such are very rare in the collection, although there is one, done in simple cross stitch, with verses and some heart and floral designs, which is inscribed *Alberta Hubbard / a gift from her cousin B. L. / May 31 1879.* Many samplers were dedicated by young children to their parents, (see opposite), and often include the verse *This I have done to let you see what care my parents took of me.* There is occasionally a more personal verse, such as the following, on a sampler of 1779:

> *Pray excuse my mean Endeavour. I'll strive to / mend and be obedient ever saith the daughter / of john taylor by ann his wife was born on Su / nday the 26 day of November at 5 o'clock in th / morning 1769. Anno Dom.*

Samplers were also made to commemorate national or local events, although few of this type are represented in the Welsh Folk Museum collection. The only nineteenth century examples referring to royal occasions are one which commemorates the Jubilee of George III, dated 3rd July 1811, and another with a long verse celebrating the coronation of Queen Victoria in 1838. The other 'royal' samplers date to the 1930s, for the jubilee of George V and the coronation of George VI. At this time, patterns for such samplers were widely published in women's magazines.

WELSH LANGUAGE SAMPLERS

The small number of surviving samplers with Welsh language inscriptions has been ascribed to the fact that English was the preferred language of schools in Wales. It was thought that copying out English verses helped the children to become familiar with the language in much the same way as reciting lessons in class. In addition, many teachers were unable to speak Welsh and this must also have had a considerable effect.

Whatever the reason for the small numbers of Welsh language inscriptions, it remains a surprising fact that of over 430 samplers collected mainly from Wales, only nineteen have any Welsh inscription and of these, none pre-dates 1821, most dating from the mid and late nineteenth century. There also seems to be no particular geographic bias. Large numbers of English language samplers were produced in strongly Welsh speaking areas and a fair proportion of the Welsh inscriptions derive from more anglicized parts of Wales.

Of the eighteen Welsh language samplers in the collection, three originate from schools in South Wales, and another was made at Willow Street School, Oswestry, Salop, though its maker was a native of Llandderfel, Gwynedd (see opposite).

Most of the verses on the Welsh samplers are biblical, the same verse from Ecclesiastes being equally popular in Welsh as it was in English - *Cofia yn awr dy Greawdwr yn nyddiau dy ieuengctid* (Remember now thy creator in the days of thy youth). Verses from

Welsh language sampler embroidered with coloured wools in cross stitch on linen canvas by Gaenor Edwards of Llandderfel, Gwynedd at Willow Street School, Oswestry, Salop.

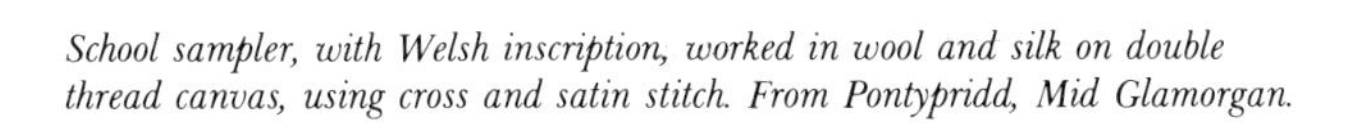

School sampler, with Welsh inscription, worked in wool and silk on double thread canvas, using cross and satin stitch. From Pontypridd, Mid Glamorgan.

Welsh language sampler, embroidered with coloured silks on woollen canvas in various stitches, including satin and cross stitch. From Peterstone Wentlloog, Gwent.

hymns are also found. It is possible that some of these were the products of Sunday Schools which had a much stronger Welsh language tradition, though none are known certainly to come from this source. The only sampler connected with a chapel commemorates a literary and musical meeting at Bethania, Port Dinorwic, Gwynedd in 1881.

One of the most attractive and original of the Welsh samplers is that embroidered by Leah Samuel in 1840 which includes a well-worked church at the top, a small cottage, naturalistic bird and floral motifs and two verses entitled *Can Mlynedd I Nawr* (A Hundred Years from Now).

The majority of the remaining Welsh language inscriptions are of the family memorial type which would more naturally be made in the language of the home. These again usually include a verse from the Bible. Margaret Williams of Whitland, Dyfed, worked one in memory of her brother David on which she embroidered a verse from Galatians chapter 3, *Da yw i wr ddwyn yr iau yn ei ieuengctid,* (It is good for a man to bear the yoke in his youth) together with her personal message *Er Cof am fy annwyl frawd* (In memory of my dear brother).

CARING FOR SAMPLERS

Cleaning samplers can present a number of problems, and all methods contain an element of risk. If in doubt, it is better to leave well alone - better a dirty sampler than a spoilt one.

The least harmful method is suction cleaning. A small vacuum cleaner, such as a Dustette, or car Hoover, with a nozzle attachment can be used. The sampler is placed flat on the table and covered with a large piece of stiff nylon net anchored firmly with some weights. This ensures that no loose threads are lost during the cleaning process. A piece of fine net or an old nylon stocking should be placed over the mouth of the nozzle which is held about 2 inches above the surface of the sampler and slowly worked over the whole area. The sampler is then turned over and the same process repeated on the reverse side. This cleaning method removes all loose dirt and debris. A soft brush can be gently used to loosen deep-set dirt particles.

A very dirty sampler can be improved by dry powder cleaning. This method will not remove stains, but works well on plain dirt by releasing the grease that binds it. Suitable powders are sodium bicarbonate, light magnesium carbonate hydrated and sepiolite, which are available from reputable chemists. ALL POWDERS MUST BE USED DRY. The sampler is placed in a shallow tray and covered with powder to a depth of ¼ inch to ½ inch and left overnight in a warm dry place, then worked over gently with a soft brush. The powder is then removed by the suction cleaning method, using the anchoring net. All the powder must be completely removed.

Sampler embroidered with coloured wools on closely-woven canvas, dated 1879, from Eglwys-fach, Dyfed.

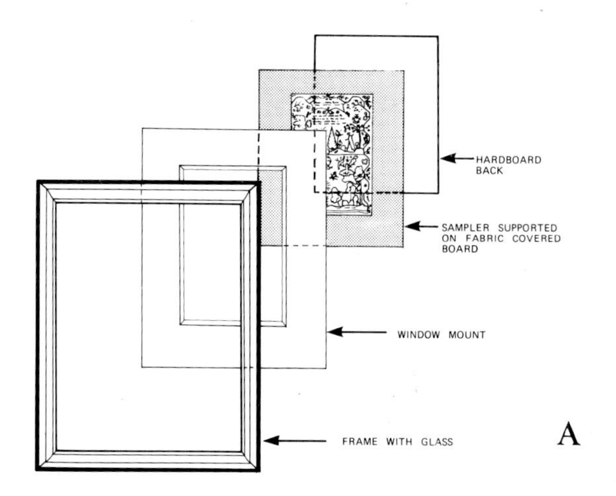

Dry cleaning with solvents is not recommended. Solvents are rarely successful in removing old stains and dirt, and they have a degreasing effect on old textiles making the fibres dry and brittle.

Washing is also not advisable, as it is an irreversible process, and should only be undertaken by trained conservators. More samplers have been ruined by being washed than by any other cause. Extensive tests must be carried out to ascertain the colour fastness and washing potential of all embroidery threads, dyes and fabrics found together on a sampler before washing is considered.

A sampler which is torn or holed should not be darned or repaired. It is essential that all of the original fabric of the sampler be retained and that nothing be added. The best way of dealing with a fragile sampler is to support it on a fabric-covered board. This will make it safe and make it look whole. Care must be taken to choose support materials which will have no harmful effects upon the sampler. The backing board can be hardboard or acid-free mounting card (museum board) ¼ inch in thickness, cut larger than the sampler. The sampler can be placed on a large backing board with wide margins which will later be covered by an acid-free window mount (diagram A) or on a board which is only marginally larger than the sampler so that the frame covers the edges of the sampler (diagram B) but does not come into direct contact with it.

The backing board is covered with a plain-weave linen or cotton of similar weight and colour to the sampler. This fabric must be washed to remove the finish, and then rinsed thoroughly in deionised or distilled water to remove all remaining traces of the detergent. Once dry, the fabric is stretched over the front of the board, matching warp and weft directions with that of the sampler. It is glued at the back of the board with PVA adhesive, taking care not to allow any glue on the front or edges of the board. The centre is marked vertically and horizontally both on the sampler and on the mount using fine lace pins and thread. The centred sampler is then pinned on the centred mount, pinning between the threads of the sampler, gently easing and adjusting the sampler and repinning as necessary. All the warps and wefts should be at right angles to each other, the threads as straight as possible, and the sampler position visually acceptable. The sampler is now stitched to the linen-covered mount using cotton thread and an oversewing stitch.

If the original frame is to be re-used, it ought to be cleaned thoroughly, treated against woodworm, and any gaps or loose joints mended and filled. All frames must have well fitting glass to eliminate the possibility of dust and insects entering. A space is left between the inside of the glass and the surface of the sampler by placing a fillet of wood or card between the two. A note giving the details of the work done and materials used is inserted in the back of the sampler in order to inform a future restorer of what has been done. On completion, the back is sealed with a sheet of hardboard and taped to keep it dust free.

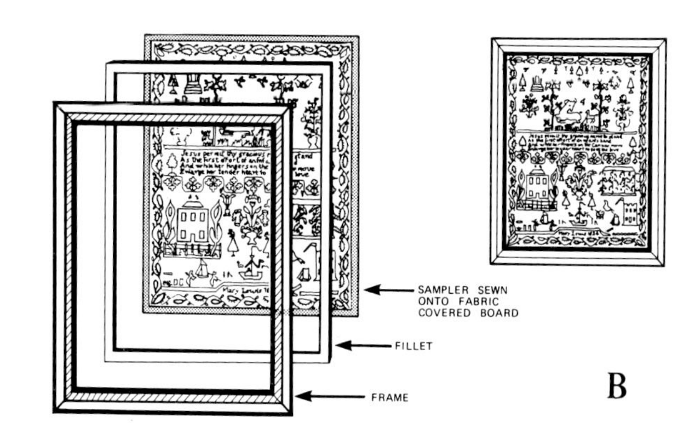

DISPLAY AND STORAGE

When displaying a sampler it is vital to show it not only to its greatest advantage, but also in conditions which will not have a detrimental influence on the specimen. The hazards of uncontrolled light, heat and humidity must be considered.

All light has a damaging effect. It causes fading and drying out of the fibres which will eventually lead to the weakening of the whole structure of the sampler. Sunlight and many fluorescent light fittings are among the most destructive forms of light, as they have a very high ultra-violet radiation content. It is advisable to hang a sampler away from direct sunlight and strong daylight, and, if it is to be artificially illuminated, to use ordinary light bulbs or low power tungsten incandescent lamps. Blinds should be drawn in strong sunlight, or a protective cover made for the sampler. The temperature and humidity must be controlled, as large fluctuations can cause slow but irreversible damage; a constant temperature of 18 - 20°C and a relative humidity of 55% - 60% is ideal. A sampler should not be hung on an outside wall, neither should it be hung on or above a direct source of heat. It is advisable to fix cork buffers, ¼ inch thick, to the back of the frame to hold the sampler away from direct contact with the wall, thus allowing air to circulate.

The glass can be cleaned with a damp cloth which has been dipped in a solution of an antistatic fabric conditioner such as Comfort or Softrinse. A dry cloth should never be used as it causes a build-up of static inside the glass which will inevitably tear the old fibres away from the sampler surface and on to the inside of the glass.

When not on display, framed samplers should be stored in a cool, dry, dark place, free of dust, smoke and fumes. Care should be taken to prevent insect and rodent infestation. Needless handling and disturbance should be avoided. The glass should be protected with card or strong bubble-pack plastic, the four corners capped with polystyrene, corrugated cardboard, or bubble-pack and the whole should be wrapped in brown paper or a dust sheet and clearly labelled.

An unframed sampler can be stored flat or rolled on to a cardboard cylinder. For flat storage, it should be laid smooth and unfolded in a tray, box or drawer with plenty of acid-free tissue paper above and below it. If rolled, a cylinder that is slightly wider than the sampler should be covered with acid-free tissue paper, then the sampler, with the right side outwards, should be rolled not too tightly around the cylinder, using plenty of acid-free tissue to protect each side. Self-adhesive tape or labels should never be used. Instead, the rolled sampler should be tied loosely with tape and identified by means of a tie-on label.

Suggestions for further reading

A. Colby, *Samplers, Yesterday and Today* (1964), Batsford.
M. B. Huish, *Samplers and Tapestry Embroideries* (1913), Longmans.
D. King, *Samplers,* Victoria and Albert Museum.
F. G. Payne, *A guide to the Collection of Samplers and Embroideries* (1939), National Museum of Wales.
N. Tarrant, *Samplers* (1973) Royal Scottish Museum.
K. M. Walton, *Samplers* (1983), Bristol City Museum.
M. Thomas, *Dictionary of Embroidery Stitches* (1934, 1981), Batsford.
K. Finch & G. Putnam, *Caring for Textiles* (1977), Barrie & Jenkins.
J. E. Leene, *Textile Conservation* (1972), Butterworth.